Newbridge Discovery Links®

Temporary Shelters

David McCoy

Newbridge

A Haights Cross Communications Company

Temporary Shelters
ISBN: 1-4007-3676-5

Program Author: Dr. Brenda Parkes, Literacy Expert
Content Reviewer: Thomas K. Fitzgerald, Professor and Head of Anthropology,
   University of North Carolina at Greensboro, Greensboro, NC

Written by David McCoy
Design assistance by Kirchoff/Wohlberg, Inc.

Newbridge Educational Publishing
11 East 26th Street, New York, NY 10010
www.newbridgeonline.com

Cover photograph: An Inuit man lights a fire in his igloo.
Table of Contents photograph: A North African woman with her child

Photo credits
Cover: B. & C. Alexander/Photo Researchers; Table of Contents page: Jonathan Blair/Corbis; Page 4:
Richard T. Nowitz/Corbis; Page 6: Newberry Library/SuperStock; Page 8: The Granger Collection,
New York; Page 9: Smithsonian American Art Museum, Washington, DC/Art Resource, NY Page 11:
Hulton Archive/Getty Images; Page 12: Nik Wheeler/Corbis; Page 14: Adrian Arbib/Corbis; Page 15:
(left) Carl & Ann Purcell/Corbis, (right) Janet Wishnetsky/Corbis; Page 16: M.E. Newman/Woodfin
Camp & Associates; Page 17: Adrian Arbib/Corbis; Page 18: Jonathon Blair/Corbis; Page 20: J.C. Carton/
Bruce Coleman Inc.; Page 21: Lauren Goodsmith/The Image Works; Page 22: B. & C. Alexander/Photo
Researchers; Page 24: (left) William Strode/Woodfin Camp & Associates, (right) William Strode/Woodfin
Camp & Associates; Page 25: (left) William Strode/Woodfin Camp & Associates, (right) William Strode/
Woodfin Camp & Associates; Page 26–27: B. & C. Alexander/Photo Researchers; Page 28: Hiroyuki Hirai/
Shigeru Ban Architects; Page 29: Hiroyuki Hirai/Shigeru Ban Architects; Page 30: Roger
Ressmeyer/Corbis

Illustration by Mike DiGiorgio, page 10; Maps by Andrew Nofsinger, pages 7, 13, 19, 23

10 9 8 7 6 5 4 3 2 1

GUIDED READING
LEVEL **S**

Table of Contents

This woman lives in a tent in a desert in Israel. What does she do in her home that you might do in yours?

A Home Is Not Always a House

Your home is probably a house or an apartment. If you move to a different home, your old home will stay where it is. Someone else will move in. That's the way many people live in today's world. They work at the same job or go to the same school all year long, so they move only once in a while.

Some people, however, move from place to place much more often. They lead a **nomadic** lifestyle. As the seasons change, they pack up their belongings and set off for a new place in search of food or work.

A permanent home like a house or apartment wouldn't work for these people. They would be looking for a new place to live all the time. How do they solve this problem?

They build homes that they can pick up and take with them when they move! Or they use **shelters** that they can put together very fast. They use materials that they can carry with them or obtain quickly and easily wherever they happen to be.

These temporary shelters provide all the comforts of home—a place to sleep and eat, a place to be with family and friends, a place to feel comfortable and safe. Aren't these the same things you get from your home?

Tipis

More than a century ago, Native American groups of the Plains followed herds of buffalo. Traveling in large groups of a hundred or more, these people depended on the animals for survival. Buffalo meat provided food. Horns and bones were made into tools. Furry hides became clothing and blankets.

The Native Americans needed shelters that were easy to set up and take down. The shelters also had to work well in all sorts of weather—cold winters, wet springs, hot summers, and windy falls. To solve this problem, the people of the Plains built **tipis**.

Cone-shaped tipis were ideal. They were movable. They shed water and snow. And a hole at the top let in fresh air.

The tipi is one of the best-known temporary shelters. It was made with wooden poles covered with buffalo skins. Families took their tipis with them year-round as they traveled the Great Plains in the United States and Canada.

Building the tipi was the job of the women in each group. They began by tying three or four poles together, standing them upright, and then added more in between. The poles were usually made from nearby pine trees.

Next, the women covered the tipi poles with buffalo hide. Pegs secured the cover into the ground. To make a doorway, they cut a large opening into the hide.

For the final step, decorations were added. Men painted the outside with designs or pictures that told the story of their hunts. Inside, women lined the tipi with more buffalo skins to keep out the wind, and made beds of hides and furs.

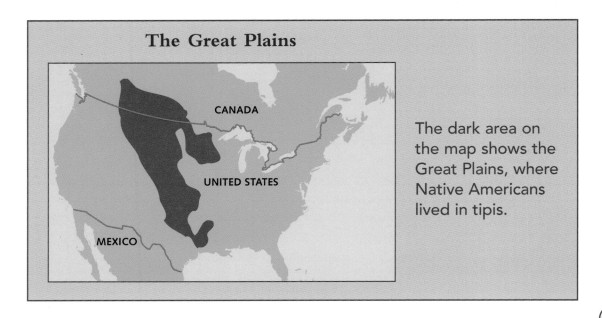

The Great Plains

CANADA

UNITED STATES

MEXICO

The dark area on the map shows the Great Plains, where Native Americans lived in tipis.

The women of the group also tended to a central fire inside each tipi. The fire provided warmth and light, and allowed them to cook food. Although it was extremely useful, the fire could also cause problems. For instance, smoke could fill up the tipi, making it difficult to breathe.

After the men hunted, women did backbreaking work. They stripped the buffalo hides, pounded them to clean and soften the hides, and finally sewed 10 to14 skins together to create the tipi cover.

To overcome this, the women made sure to leave an opening at the tipi's top, which allowed smoke to escape. It was covered with two **smoke flaps** that could be opened as needed. On rainy, windy, or bitterly cold days, they made sure to close the flaps tightly so that everyone stayed warm and dry inside.

Women were responsible for choosing the location of the village campsites. They usually faced the tipis toward the east, away from the wind.

How many people live with you in your home? Generally, Plains people lived with many family members. A mother, father, sons, daughters, grandparents, and even aunts and uncles would all live together in a single tipi. You can understand why some had to be built quite large!

During the hot summers, it was often a problem to cook inside the family shelter. So, the Plains women would quickly pitch a special kitchen tipi nearby. They rolled up the cover to about knee-height to allow cool air to sweep in underneath. Sometimes, they completely cut away the bottom part if the covering was worn and old.

Kitchen Tipi

Old tipis were sometimes given a new life as kitchen tipis. They were very simple and could be taken down quickly if a sudden storm came up. How did women change the tipi design to help the flow of air?

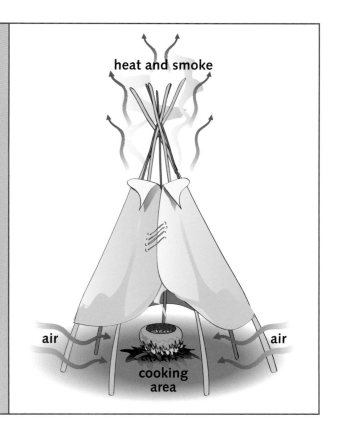

heat and smoke

air

air

cooking area

Tipis could be taken down very quickly. The women wrapped the cover around its poles. Then, they loaded the tipi onto a device called a **travois.** It was like a sled made from tipi poles, and it was used to carry their belongings. Dogs or horses dragged each travois to the next hunting ground.

Today, Native Americans of the Plains live in homes just like yours. Sometimes at special gatherings they set up tipis to live in for a day or two. It is one of the ways that they celebrate their past and how their people were able to survive.

The travois was used to carry a family's belongings. Sometimes young children or very old adults climbed aboard to ride to the next spot.

Gers

For thousands of years, the people in Mongolia, Kazakhstan, and other parts of Central Asia have lived as herders. They move with their sheep, cattle, goats, horses, and camels whenever they need new pastures. The herders live on **steppes**—high plains that stretch below soaring mountains.

Strong winds can easily knock down square buildings. The ger's circular shape helps it withstand high-speed winds, which slip around the shelter's curved walls.

These people need shelters that are easy to heat and can withstand 90-mile-per-hour winds during the long winters. However, in the summer, the same shelters also have to let in air but still protect families from the scorching sun, heat, and winds.

To overcome this problem, the herders build round tents called **gers.** Ger means "home" in Mongolian. Gers are also known as yurts. Gers provide a comfortable home in some of the highest, bleakest parts of the world.

A ger has curved walls and a domed roof. Air moves easily within this circular tent because there are no corners to block the flow. This airflow keeps the home cool in the summer and warm in the winter.

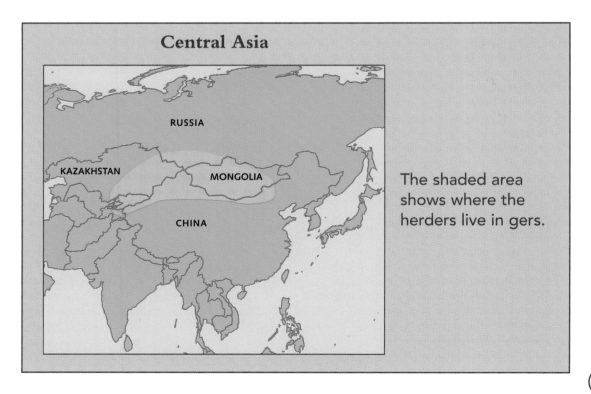

Central Asia

RUSSIA

KAZAKHSTAN

MONGOLIA

CHINA

The shaded area shows where the herders live in gers.

Unlike tipis, gers are built by men. First, they make walls by tying together sticks in a lattice pattern. This design has crisscrossed diagonal lines. Each section of the wall is called a **hana** in Mongolian.

Next, they tie several hanas together in a circle that connects on either side of a door frame. They use more sticks to make a dome-shaped roof. Finally, they stretch thick felt mats, made from sheep wool, over the frame. The mats are either weighed down with stones or tied into place.

If wool can keep a sheep warm on the outside, think how cozy the ger feels inside, under the wool felt cover. Herders use as many as eight layers of felt in the winter, when temperatures can dip 50 degrees below zero Fahrenheit. Strong winds make it feel even colder.

A man ties several two-meter-high lattice walls together in a circle to create a frame for the ger.

In summer, herders might only use one layer of felt, peeling the others off as you would take off a jacket when it gets too warm. Using layers helps them solve the problem of changing temperatures. They can also roll up the bottom of the felt, to allow air to enter through the latticework walls.

Like a tipi, a ger has a smoke hole at the top that also lets in fresh air. For the Mongolian people, this hole represents a "sun gate." It connects the inside of their home to the larger universe outside.

Herders hang a decorated felt flap over the entrance of their ger. It serves as a door during the day.

Gers always face the south, to let in sunlight during the day.

Gers are usually kept comfortable and neat. Every item has its proper place.

Inside a ger, a pit stands in the center. It's used for building a fire for cooking and keeping the ger warm in the winter. Colorful rugs hang from the walls. Others are spread around the floor for sitting and sleeping. There are also storage places for utensils, food, clothing, and extra rugs.

After months of use, the area around a ger can get dirty. Cleaning it is a family task. First, the owners move their furniture and other belongings outside. Then, they remove the felt cover. Finally, family members take up positions around the walls. They simply lift the ger and move it to a clean patch of ground!

Herders began building bigger gers after they got camels, which were strong enough to carry their temporary shelters from place to place.

A man can usually put up a ger in less than an hour. It takes about the same amount of time to take it down. The lattice sections fold flat for easy transport. When herders travel to a new place, the entire ger—the felt covering and all the wood pieces—is loaded onto the back of a horse or camel and carried to the next destination.

Gers are good shelters for nomads in Asia, who need to take their homes with them wherever they go.

The existing desert sand provides a soft "floor" for sitting, walking, and sleeping.

Desert Tents

Like the nomads in Central Asia, many North Africans live as herders. They lead their camels, cattle, goats, and sheep across the Sahara Desert in search of food and water. They often travel hundreds of miles from one fertile area to another in the dry desert.

The Sahara's climate is very different from that in the Great Plains or Central Asia. Summers are very long and extremely hot. Daytime temperatures reach 100°F or higher! Strong winds also sweep through the region, stirring up fierce sandstorms.

The people of the Sahara need shelters that are temporary—like tipis and gers—but that will help them cope with the climate. To solve this problem, they live in desert tents.

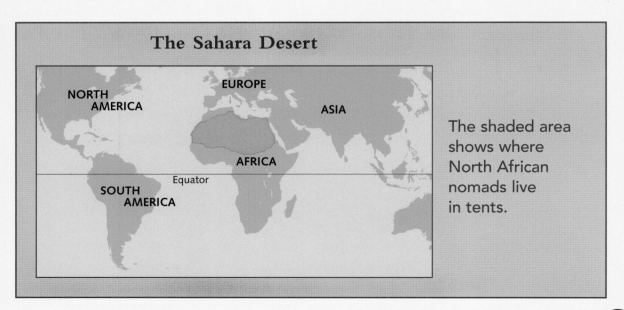

The Sahara Desert

NORTH AMERICA

EUROPE

ASIA

AFRICA

Equator

SOUTH AMERICA

The shaded area shows where North African nomads live in tents.

Inside a desert tent, rugs and mats like these are used for sleeping.

Desert tents look different from the kind of tent you might use on a camping trip. Low and wide, they provide shade under the hot sun.

During the heat of the day, people open the sides to let in fresh air, and then close them at night. The sides are also closed during sandstorms, just as you would shut a window to keep out rain.

Nomads in the Sahara Desert make covers for their tents from cloth, cattle hides, and even palm-tree leaves. The frames are made with wood, which they get from the few trees that grow in the area. Inside the tent, woven mats make up the beds. A few clay pots are used for cooking and eating.

When it's time to head to a new area, the nomads take down the frames and load them, along with the cover, onto camels. It's easy to put the tent up again quickly at the next location. Nomadic families move without wasting the resources around them!

The cover for this tent is made of cloth woven from goat or camel hair. Inside, a woman makes tea.

Igloos

In the Arctic today, the Inuit (also known as Eskimos) live in modern homes in towns and villages. Sometimes, however, the Inuit practice the ways of the past, when their people were nomads.

This far north, summers are short and winters are long. Ice and snow cover the land. Temperatures can dip to –100°F if you factor in the wind chill.

> A hole in the roof lets in sunlight to light an igloo.

Like the Native Americans of the Great Plains, the Inuit were hunters. Wandering in search of caribou, seals, polar bears, and fish, they also needed temporary shelters.

However, trees to make wooden poles or frames are not available in the Arctic. How did the Inuit solve this problem? There was plenty of snow and ice around. So, they used them as building materials to make **igloos**.

An igloo has an interesting shape. It looks like the top half of a ball. The Arctic wind easily blows over its curved surface. If the igloo was shaped like a box, the wind would hit it head on, causing damage.

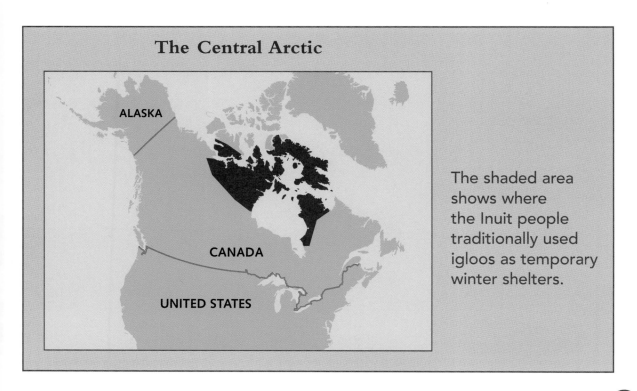

The Central Arctic

ALASKA

CANADA

UNITED STATES

The shaded area shows where the Inuit people traditionally used igloos as temporary winter shelters.

Imagine that you are an Inuit man. You can build a small igloo in several hours. First, you must find the right kind of snow. Not too hard. Not too soft.

Next, you dig a circle into the ground about ten feet wide. Stepping inside it, you place a layer of snow blocks along the circle. Then, you pile several layers on top of the first, making sure each layer is slightly smaller than the one beneath. You gently tilt them inward to form a dome.

Closing up the igloo's roof traps you inside. So, you cut a small doorway with a knife.

An Inuit man uses a long knife or saw to cut blocks of snow that are about 1 meter long, 60 centimeters wide, and 30 centimeters thick.

There are still many cracks between the blocks of ice. What's the perfect material to fix this problem? Soft snow! You place it into the cracks, making an airtight seal. Then, you cut a small hole at the top for the chimney. If you can find a piece of clear ice, you use it as a window along the wall.

Finally, you dig a trench that stretches outward from the doorway. You can construct a curved wall over it, forming a tunnel that leads up to the entrance. The tunnel keeps harsh winds from rushing into the igloo.

Family members can crawl in and out of the doorway to enter or exit the igloo.

Inside the igloo, you use more snow to build platforms for eating and sleeping. Covers of caribou fur will make the beds warm and soft. You cut shelves into the walls to store utensils.

A small fire gives off enough heat to keep people comfortable. But it doesn't get hot enough to melt the solid walls of ice.

Very few Inuit lived in igloos all year long. In the summer, they slept in tents made of skins. Unlike tipis, gers, or desert tents, igloos were not movable. But that didn't matter. There would be plenty of ice and snow at the next spot.

Igloos can range in size, but most are built to house a single family.

Cardboard Shelters

Many of the shelters you have read about in this book have been around for hundreds of years. But cardboard shelters are so new most people have never heard of them.

A Japanese architect named Shigeru Ban first began to use cardboard tubes in the 1980s. He needed cheap building materials for an exhibition he was designing. The result was so successful, Ban declared that cardboard was an improved form of wood!

> Shigeru Ban's simple cardboard tube shelter is very attractive. How do you think it feels inside?

In the 1990s, Ban worked with the United Nations and other organizations. He used leftover cardboard tubes to build temporary shelters for people who lost their homes in earthquakes in Japan in 1995 and Turkey in 1999. He also sent tubes to people in need in Rwanda.

Today, Ban uses cardboard tubes to create temporary and permanent buildings, including his own weekend house outside of Tokyo. A temporary cardboard shelter can be built quickly and cheaply. Crates filled with heavy sandbags serve as its **foundation.** Sturdy walls are made of the cardboard tubes. A canvas spread across the top makes a roof.

Ban's cardboard shelters can be set up and taken down quickly by people who know nothing about building houses. And you can recycle the shelters!

Like tipis, gers, tents, and igloos, cardboard shelters are made from materials that are easy to get. As the population rises around the world, construction materials such as wood, steel, and stone become scarce. More and more, people look for new or different materials to build temporary homes and permanent ones, too.

For instance, instead of throwing old tires and tin cans away, some people in the United States have used them to build permanent houses. Clay and other materials hold them together. In Arizona, other people have built houses using bales of straw.

No matter what a shelter is made of, no matter where it is, and whether it's permanent or temporary, if it provides protection and comfort, it's home.

This house in Taos, New Mexico, is made from old tires and other recycled materials.

Glossary

foundation: the bottom on which a house is built

ger: round tent with domed roof made of felt (or skins) and stretched over a latticework frame

hana: lattice wall section of a ger

igloo: shelter made of snow and ice that is shaped like a dome

nomadic: wandering from place to place rather than living in a permanent home

shelter: something that covers or protects from weather or danger

smoke flap: top flap of a tipi. Attached poles open and close a flap to let out smoke or to keep rain and wind from coming inside.

steppe: vast, level, treeless land in southeastern Europe or Central Asia with extreme temperature range

tipi: cone-shaped shelter made of animal hide (or canvas in modern times). It was originally used by Plains Native Americans.

travois: French term for a sled made with two tipi poles, tied together at one end, pulled by a horse or dog

Index

Websites

To learn more about temporary shelters, go to:
www.epa.gov/glnpo/native/2001/diagram.pdf
www.chaingang.org/yurtquest/
www.netscapades.com/franklintrail/igloobuilding.html